Never Stand Between a Cowboy and His Spittoon

Laughs from the Old West Press

LEO W. BANKS

WitWorks

WitWorks™
a funny little division of arizona highways books

2039 West Lewis Avenue, Phoenix, Arizona 85009
Telephone: (602) 712-2200
Website: www.witworksbooks.com

Publisher WIN HOLDEN
Managing Editor BOB ALBANO
Associate Editor EVELYN HOWELL
Associate Editor P. K. MCMAHON
Art Director MARY WINKELMAN VELGOS
Photography Director PETER ENSENBERGER
Production Director CINDY MACKEY

Library of Congress Catalog Number — 00-110192
ISBN — 1-893860-11-6

Never Stand Between a Cowboy and His Spittoon
FIRST EDITION, published in 2001.

Printed in the United States.

Book design by BILLIE BISHOP
Cover photography © CARLTON'S PHOTOGRAPHIC, INC.

Humor —
Stereotypes and All

Humor helps define us. It reinforces the bound-
aries of what is acceptable and outrageous, what is modern
and out-dated, what is crass and classy. Besides laughs,
humor tells us about the behavior and traits of men, women
and children and the roles they fill.

In the jokes selected for this book, all of which were
"fillers" taken from newspapers published before Arizona
became a state in 1912, you'll encounter the prejudices and
assumptions of the time.

Men usually are depicted as dumb, drunken goldbricking
fools, and darn happy to be that way until they marry. Then
a veil of misery descends over their lives, which become
consumed with outrageous bills from the dressmaker,
mother-in-law trouble, and henpeckery.

As for women, the only thing they want more than a man
and marriage is to trash their female rivals with cold, slicing
remarks. Oh, yes. They also have a need — apparently genetic
— to conceal their true age.

We make no apologies for presenting these stereotypes,
which, in today's world would draw letters of protest.

Introduction

In the first place, and most importantly, they're laugh-out-loud funny. But they also represent what Arizonans were reading in Territorial times, and in that way, they tell us how much things have changed, and how little.

Insurance agents are still chinning people, driving them crazy.

Government jobs hardly qualify as work in the view of taxpayers.

Tramps are still looking for handouts, politicians are crooked, and even a good doctor will kill you.

When you read about Alakali Ike, a recurring character used by early humorists, you'll understand something about how Westerners were caricatured as unshaven, uncouth, and unacceptable.

But it's still funny, because like every other joke in this book, it contains a germ of truth about how we are, and who we are. Laughing is always good, and laughing at ourselves is even better.

— LEO W. BANKS
Tucson, Arizona

Courtship, Romance, and Jilted Love

She (softly): "I shall never forget this night — and the ball."

He (tenderly): "Tell me why."

She: "And that last waltz."

He: "You delight me!"

She: "And you!"

He: "You entrance me! Then I have impressed you?"

She (more softly than ever): "Yes, you've smashed two of my toes."

How he caught
the banker's daughter:

"I must sneeze
whenever I look at you."

"But why, captain?"

"Because everybody must
sneeze when looking
at the sun."

SHE: "What color eyes do you admire, brown or blue?"

HE: "I can't see well enough in this light."

TOM: "You ought not to consider your case as hopeless just because she said no."

JACK: "To be perfectly exact, what she said was 'rats.' "

Tommy (to Dudely Canesucker):
"Why don't you stand on one leg when
you come here?"

Dudely Canesucker: "Why — what a
queer question."

Tommy: "Well, sister Alice said
that you are a regular goose, and
all the geese I ever saw
stood on one leg."

Strange thrills and qualms
my spirit move,

I ask myself the question,

Is it the pang of
nascent love,

Or is it indigestion?

Mrs. Gradley: "I saw young Bingley on the street today. He was drunk, and you know, he hadn't touched a drop since he promised to reform for Clara Jenkins' sake. That cruel girl has broken the engagement or else —

Mr. Gradley: "She married him!"

Old Deacon Amos Twitterworth,
who keeps the village store,

Has courted Miss Susanna Chick
for twenty years or more,

Whene'er he calls, they chat about
the weather and the crops,

And then she sighs, and he sighs,
and the conversation stops,

Until at last he rises,
as her gran'father's clock strikes eight,

"Now, who'd 'a' thought," he says to her,
"that it had grown so late."

"Old Gayboy has married again."

"You don't tell me so."

*"Yes, and he married
a right young girl, forty years
younger than he is."*

*"Well, I declare! His other wife
died six months ago and he
went on so at the grave that
I expected he'd lose his mind."*

*"Well, you see your
prediction has come to pass."*

MISS PINKERLY: "I hope you will see me in a new gown when you call again."

YOUNG TUTTER: "When do you expect to get it, Miss Clara?"

MISS PINKERLY: "Oh, not for several weeks!"

MICROBES MAY BE IN KISSES,

AS SCIENTISTS DECLARE,

BUT WHAT DO YOUTHS
AND MISSES,

WHO KNOW JUST WHAT
THE BLISS IS,

FOR BLOOMING
MICROBES CARE?

Maud: "I don't see how you can stand being engaged to a man who has to work nights."

Marie: "He comes to see me afternoons."

Maud: "Pshaw! How insipid! When he's gone you must feel as though you've been to a matinee."

"What is it, do you suppose,
that keeps the moon
in place and prevents it from
falling?" asked Mary.

"I think it must be the beams,"
said Charlie, softly.

*She shrank away coyly
at his approach.*

*"Are we alone?" she faltered
in apprehension.*

*"I don't know," he answered.
"You might sing a few
selections and make sure."*

GOODFELLO: "WASN'T
THAT NICEFELLO
WHO JUST ASKED FOR YOU?"

SWEET GIRL: "I TOLD THE MAID TO
TELL HIM I WAS NOT AT HOME."

GOODFELLO: "SUPPOSE HE FINDS OUT
THAT YOU WERE?"

SWEET GIRL: "I'LL TELL HIM
I THOUGHT IT WAS YOU."

He bore each passing
fad or whim,

No wish met his denial,

Her lightest word
was law to him,

He stood all test and trial.

Even whispers of her
broken oath,

He scorned as idle rumors,

But he gave her back her
plighted troth,

The day she put on bloomers.

*She talked so well
on women's rights,*

*That all the fellows
got scared and flew,*

*And now, alas,
she has her way,*

And paddles her own canoe.

"Mr. Dunguss," said the young man, twirling his hat nervously. "I have called to ask you for your daughter, Phoebe. I am not rich, but I have good business prospects and . . . "

"Young man," interrupted the man (Father), "before we discuss the matter further, will you oblige me with a loan of five dollars?"

"I will not," replied the youth firmly.

"Then take her, my boy," said Mr. Dunguss. "You've got more sense than I thought you had."

"I wish to propose for the
hand of your daughter."

"Which of them, young man?
Which of them?"

"Well, I don't know.
Now, in confidence, which of
them would you advise
a fellow to take?"

SOON 'MID THE ROCKS
UPON THE SHORE,

WITH GRIEF THAT PIERCES
THROUGH YOU,

YOU'LL HEAR THOSE ECHOED WORDS
ONCE MORE,

"I'LL BE A SISTER TO YOU."

Mildred: "I believe Jack Scribley is a member of the press club."

Millicent: "He must be, to judge by his actions with Mable in the conservatory last evening."

He: "Will you be mine — mine until death do us part?"

She: "I don't know about that. You look as if you might live a good many years."

Miss Keane to handsome young
physician at the ball:
*"Oh, doctor, how do you do?
You look killing this evening."*

Young physician (quietly):
*"Thank you, but I'm not.
I'm off-duty, don't you know."*

CHOLLIE: "What a bwute old Goltwox is! Told me if I did not stop hanging awound his daughter he would bwain me. He meant unbwain me, don't you think?"

YABSLEY: "No, I don't think he did."

One: "She was engaged to eight men
last summer and is now
gradually breaking them off."

The other: "Gracious! What awful
chances the last man runs."

She said, "I cannot
kiss you, sir,"

While to her cheeks
the color flew,

"Well, never mind,"
he said to her,

"You just keep still
and I'll kiss you."

Cora: "I expect Mr. Merritt
this evening, so don't hide any of your
fireworks in the parlor."

Little Johnnie: "I guess not. You two
spark so much, you'd be sure
to set them off."

WE STUMBLE ON THE GIFTS WE PRIZE,

ALL OTHER THINGS ABOVE,

FOR EVER SINCE THE WORLD BEGAN,

WE'VE FALLEN INTO LOVE.

Young Jefferson: *"You look sweet enough to kiss in that dress."*

Elaine: *"I have several more just like it."*

"Although I am a septuagenarian,
remember I'm a millionaire.
Could you learn to love me?
Am I too old for you?"

"On the contrary. You are too young."

Burglars Must Work While Others Sleep

———◆✦◆———

"It is evident," said the judge, "that you shot this man with malice aforethought."

"No, I didn't, yer honor. It wuz with plain buckshot."

Arizona tourist (solemnly): "My friend, have you, in your sinful and ungodly life, ever enjoyed unalloyed happiness?"

Alkali Ike: "Looky yere, stranger. Do you reckon I've lived in Arizona all these years and never participated in a lynchin' bee?"

He made a great name
for himself,

But 'twas another's name,
you see,

And so the jury sent him up,

seven years for forgery.

Burglar (soliloquizing):
"Yer neva hear a good word
for a housebreaker. People
never takes into consideration
that we're obliged to be out
in all kinds o' weather, an'
that most o' the work has to
be done while lazy folks is
sound asleep in their beds."

Police: "State how the trouble
originated."

Accused: "We was holdin' a debatin'
society and I had the floor and
he called me a liar."

Police: "What followed?"

Accused: "From that time until we were
arrested we both had the floor."

CHARLEY BOY: "Any news regarding the robbery?"

OFFICER O'BRIEN: "Naw, but they found the tray of diamonds."

CHARLEY BOY: "Where did they find it?"

OFFICER O'BRIEN: "They found it in a pack of cards, sonny."

Banker: "Well, our cashier has skipped."

Mrs. B: "What, that modest unassuming gentleman? Why, I thought he was positively shy.

Banker: "He was shy — fifty thousand dollars."

"Gimme your watch and chain," said the train robber.

"Great scott," sobbed the Pullman porter, "ain't there no ethics in our profession."

One of the local justices
of the peace identified the prisoner
at the bar as an old offender.

Justice: "What is your name?"

Prisoner: "Sam Jackson."

Justice: "Three years ago
when you were up before me, you said
your name was John Smith."

Prisoner: "Yes, but that was an entirely
different case."

"You are charged with having voted five times in one day," said the judge sternly.

"I am charged, am I?" repeated the prisoner. "I expected to be paid for it."

Seedy Samson: *"You see, your honor, I was intoxicated with joy over . . ."*

Judge: *"The intoxication may have been of joy, but the odor is the odor of alcohol. Thirty days."*

JUDGE: "Did the prisoner offer
any resistance?"

OFFICER: "Only five dollars,
yer honor."

"Thickhed's ignorance has got him in a box at last."

"Has, huh? What kind of box?"

"Jury box."

Lawyer: "Then I understand you'd swear, witness, that the parties came to high words?"

Witness: "No, sir. Wot I sat is, the words were particularly low."

A couple of jailbirds were drinking
together when one of them
took out his watch.

"Bless me!" exclaimed his astonished
companion, "you've got a watch."

"Looks like it."

"And how much did it cost you?"

"Six months."

Life, Death, and Other Annoyances

TRAVELER: "Who's the close-mouthed individual in the corner? He hasn't spoken for ten minutes."

STOREKEEPER: "He's jus' waitin' fer Pete t' come back with th' spittoon."

Tired Traveler: "I has got
a position, Weary."

Weary Walker: "What! Has you forgotten
th' sacred traditions of our
brotherhood?"

Tired Traveler: "Naw. It's a government
position."

Arizona horse trader:
"Gentlemen, I can't lie about a horse. He's blind in one eye."

Buyer, handing over the money:
"You were honest enough to tell me of this animal's defect, I'll take it."

Horse trader, stuffing the money in his pocket: *"Oh, I forgot to mention. He's also blind in the other eye."*

MRS. BAKER: "Here's an account of another man robbed in broad daylight."

BAKER: "Had a prescription filled, I suppose."

BANKER (visiting the ranch): "I suppose that's the hired man."

RANCHER (who has visited banks): "No, that's the first vice-president in charge of cows."

Three old ladies couldn't
hear very well. One day they
met on the street. The first lady
said, "Windy, isn't it?"

The second lady said, "No,
it's Thursday."

The third one said, "Me, too.
Let's go get a drink."

*"Madam," said the tramp,
"take back yer loaf of bread.
I return it unbroken."*

"What's the matter?"

*"It brings back too many sad
memories. I can't tech it."*

*"Does it," she asked gently,
"make you think of the bread
your mother used to bake?"*

*"No. It makes me think of
when I was doin' time
on the rock piles."*

Medical examiner for insurance company: "You appear to be in a very weak, nervous, depressed physical condition."

Applicant for insurance: "Yes. Your agents have been chinning at me for six months."

"How is it, Mr. Brown," said
the mill owner to the farmer,
"that when I came to measure
those five barrels of apples
I bought from you, I found
them nearly a barrel short?"

"That's very strange,
for I put them up in some of
your very own flour barrels."

"Ahem! You did, eh?
Well, perhaps I made a mistake.
Fine weather, isn't it?"

"This seems a very healthy
spot, my man," said the tourist
to the Arizona cowboy.
"I suppose people don't die
here very often."

"No, sir. They only die once."

Coroner: "It is a very unhappy occurrence that you should run over this old lady and kill her."

Arizona stagecoach driver: "Very. This makes my thirteenth, and I feel that number'll bring me bad luck."

Mammoth drops of water,

Little chunks of grease,

Make the soup for which we pay,

Fifty cents apiece.

"Jenkinson is a terrible
pessimist, isn't he?"

"He used to be, but the hard times have
pleased him so much that he
rather takes a hopeful
view of things lately."

Mr. Mulhooly: *"Phwat fur are yez makin' such a noise on that pianny? Yer drivin' me distracted wid yer racket, an' my head is achin' loik it wud split in two places."*

Daughter: *"Them new neighbors nixt door has been complainin' of my playin.'"*

Mr. Mulhooly: *"Begorra, hammer harder!"*

HOTEL GUEST, TENTH STORY:
"What's this rope coiled up in
the corner for?"

PORTER: "Dat's fo' use
in case of fiah, sah."

**GUEST, AFTER LOOKING
OUT THE WINDOW TO
THE SIDEWALK:**
"Oh, I see. Very convenient.
If a man objects to being
burned to death
he can hang himself."

An old Irish woman
approaches a bank clerk

Clerk: "Do you want to draw
or deposit?"

Woman: "Noah, I don't.
Oi wants ter put some in."

The clerk opens the book and indicates
the line for her signature.

Woman: "Above it or below it?"

Clerk: "Just above it."

Woman: "Me whole name?"

Clerk: "Yes. Yes."

Woman: "Before Oi was married?"

Clerk: "No, just as it is now."

Woman: "Oi can't write."

HE NAMED HIS LAYING HEN MACDUFF

AND WHEN AT EARLY DAWN,

SHE CACKLED LOUD, HE CRIED IN GLEE,

"LAY ON, MACDUFF, LAY ON."

Domestic at miner's house: "Oh, please,
mum, what shall I do?
Half the soup is spilt and the boarders is
at the table."

Mrs. Slimdiet (firmly): "Empty the box
of red pepper into what's left.
There'll be enough then."

Eastern stranger: "What are they lynching him for?"

Quick Drop Dan: "Attempted suicide."

Eastern Stranger: "They might just as well let him kill himself."

Quick Drop Dan: "No, siree. The boys out here don't believe in a fellow being selfish."

Miss East (at an Arizona ball): "Pardon
me for treading on
your toe, sir."

Alkali Ike (gallantly): "Not a-tall,
I assure you! Pardon me for
havin' a toe."

**"Ah," exclaimed the cannibal
chief, smacking his lips,
"what kind of minister was that
we had for dinner?"**

**"Your excellency," replied his
companion, "I should say he
was a prime minister."**

In order to save time,
the young man who had come
for a marriage license
handed in a card containing
the names of Nokkolaus
Blohockenschimpff and Varina Morff.

"These are the names of the parties,
I suppose," said the county clerk.

"Yes, sir."

"You are Mr. Bl . . . Bl . . ."

"Yes, sir."

"May I ask how you pronounce
that name?"

"Yes, sir. Two coughs and a sneeze."

Chapter Three

Weary Willis: "Madam,
I crave your mercy. I'm hungry
enough to eat a dog."

Madam: "All right. I'll just
unchain him."

*A frontier doctor was called out
to an Indian reservation
to help deliver a baby.
He went, and the baby came.
It had red hair. The doctor
thought this odd, and knowing
that settlers had been passing
the area, he asked the new
mother, "Did the father
have red hair?"*

*"I don't know," said the squaw.
"He didn't take off his hat."*

Chapter Three

THE GLORIOUS CHARGE OF
THE LIGHT BRIGADE,

BY TENNYSON FAMOUSLY SUNG,

IS NOTHING TO THAT WHICH
MY DOCTOR MADE,

FOR TAKING A LOOK AT MY TONGUE.

Mrs. P to the new servant:
"I suppose, Bridget, you heard my
husband and I conversing rather
earnestly this morning."

Bridget: "Indade, I did, mum."

Mrs. P: "I hope you did not
consider that anything
unusual was going on."

Bridget: "Niver a bit, mum.
I wunst had a husband myself, mum,
and niver a day passed that the
neighbors didn't believe one or
the other of us would be kilt entoirely."

Jones: "That's all nonsense about eating meat being injurious to your health. My ancestors for hundreds of years ate meat."

Vegetarian: "Yes, and where are they now? Dead, aren't they?"

Drifter looking for ranch work:
"How do you expect a man
to be a Christian on
a dollar a day?"

Ranch Owner: "I don't see
how he can afford to be
anything else."

An Unreasonable Request

Esther (to her betrothed): "Do learn to skate, George. I'm sure you would look lovely on ice."

George (a young and rising undertaker): "Look lovely on ice! Thank you. I'm in no hurry about that."

A CHARMING YOUNG BELLE
OF THE SIOUX,

STOOPED OVER TO LACE UP
HER SHIOUX,

BUT SHE SAID AS SHE LACED,

"I MUST HAVE THESE REPLACED,

FOR I SEE THEY NO LONGER
WILL DIOUX."

PROF. SMITH: "No one
can conceive of the slow and
awful lapse of geological time."

BROWN: "I don't know.
I've had a carpenter
working for me by the day."

She: *"How fearful it must be for a great singer to know that she has lost her voice."*

He: *"It's much more torturing when she doesn't know it."*

Chapter Three

THERE'S HEADS AND HEADS AND
HEAD AND HEADS,

LONG HEADS, ROUND HEADS AND FLATS,

SOME HEADS ARE MADE TO CARRY BRAINS,

AND SOME JUST CARRY HATS.

How to Make a Family Scrapbook

———◆·>·◆·<·◆———

"Sheriff, you'd better lock
me up. I jush hit my wife over
th' head with a club."

"Did you kill her?"

"Don't think sho. Thash why
I wanna be locked up."

WHEN I WAS YOUNG,
MY WIFE SHE CALLED ME DARLING,
DUCKY AND SWEET,

BUT NOWADAYS MY PET NAME IS

"WHY DON'T YOU WIPE YOUR FEET."

Wife: *"My first husband was a great fellow to get other people into scrapes."*

Husband: *"He must have had me in mind when he died."*

"My wife is getting awfully strenuous," remarked Whiffles. "Yesterday she broke a plate over my head. Would you advise me what to do?"

"Well," replied Sniffles, "you might buy cast-iron plates."

"So you are mad at your husband. Are you going home to your mother?"

"No. I shan't do anything to please him again as long as I live."

Mrs. Norris: *"In this little book I have written down most of the little incidents of our married life."*

Old Man Bonder: *"Ah, sort of a family scrap-book, eh?"*

Wife: "I am afraid you
are not enjoying dinner.
What are you thinking of?"

Husband: "I was thinking
that there must be misprints
in your cookbook."

Irate Husband: "I wish you were somewhere where I could never see you again."

Patient Wife: "Well, that's equivalent to wishing I were in heaven."

WIFE, AS SHE AND HER HUSBAND START FOR THE CITY: "That necktie of yours is horribly loud."

HUSBAND: "Well, no one will hear it with your hat in the neighborhood."

"Binks has got one of those
talking machines."

"A phonograph?"

"No, a wife."

Police Inspector: "It was very plucky
of you, ma'am, to have set upon
the burglar and so ably captured him,
but need you have injured him
to the extent of necessitating his
removal to a hospital?"

Lady: "How did I know it was a burglar?
I'd been waiting up for three hours for
my husband. I thought it was him!"

*A woman asked a farmer
— all the while being certain
that her husband could hear —
if it was true that the bull
yonder in the pasture could,
as she put it, make love a
number of times a day.*

*"Sure can," whined the farmer.
But as the woman turned to
give her husband a self-satisfied
see-there gesture, the farmer
added, "But of course with a
different cow each time."*

Merchant: "Mr. Remington, you have ruined me, simply ruined me!"

Stenographer: "How so, sir?"

Merchant: "I dictated a letter yesterday to 'Mrs. Ferguson, Hotel Woodmore, Suite One,' and you began it, 'Mrs. Ferguson, Hotel Woodmore, Sweet One,' and Mrs. Ferguson forwarded the letter to my wife."

"I was just struck with an idea," said Gus de Jay.

"Well, if it's one of your own," replied Gus's father, "I guess you ain't likely to be black and blue from it."

The Art of Insults

He: "A fellow called me
a donkey the other day."

She: "Didn't you feel
like kicking him?"

Mr. Newlywed: *"Here's the two dollars for your fee, sir. I suppose you will want to kiss the bride."*

Mayor: *"Er, I say, suppose you keep the two dollars and we'll call it square."*

The Dear Creatures

Maud: "Your fiancé called on me last night."

Mabel: "Indeed?"

Maud: "Yes. Guess what he said to me?"

Mabel: "I haven't the least notion."

Maud: "He said, 'I wish that I dared to kiss you.'"

Mabel (confidently): "But he didn't do it."

Maud: "How do you know?"

Mabel (sweetly): "There are limits even to heroism."

MISS SHARPE: "Oh, how do you do, Mr. Sissy? You are not looking very well."

MR. SISSY: "No, I have a cold or something in my head."

MISS SHARPE (calmly): "It must be a cold."

The Art of Insults

Patrick Rogan's face was
an offense to the landscape.
Next to his poverty, it was the most
conspicuous part of him.

Irish neighbor: "An' how are ye, Pat?"

Patrick: "Moighty bad entoirely.
It's shtarvation that's shtaring me
in the face."

Irish neighbor: "Is that so?
I'm sure it can't be very pleasant
for ayther of yez."

Minnie: *"Capt. Foster has never paid me any attention before. But he danced with me four times last night."*

Maud: *"Oh, well, it was a charity ball, you remember."*

She: "They say this photograph doesn't do me justice."

Her younger brother: "Well, I wouldn't feel hurt if they do say so. Justice should always be tempered with mercy."

Chappie: *I'm going to get square with Clara. I'm going to send her one of those comic valentines, a hideous grinning monkey, don't you know."*

Prunella: *"Why not call on her in person?"*

**TAILOR (to stout customer):
"Have the kindness to put your
finger on this bit of tape, sir.
Just here. I'll be round you
in a minute."**

Friend: "What are you going to do with
this immense revolver?"

Dolly Simple: "I'm tired of life,
me deah fellah, and I'm going to
blow me bwains out."

Friend: "Pshaw! Why don't you just take
a pinch of snuff and sneeze?"

Chapter Five

EASTERN TINHORN: "Can you tell me where Mr. Greencorn's cottage is?"

ARIZONA FARM BOY: "I can for a nickel."

TINHORN: "Okay, here's a nickel."

FARM BOY: "It burned down."

Kids — Smart and Smart-alecky

Teacher: "What is a peninsula?"

Saloon boy: "A point of land extending into the water."

Teacher: "Good. What is a strait?"

Saloon Boy: "Ace, king, queen, jack and a ten-spot."

Teacher: "Why did you put that pin in my chair?"

Bad Boy: "Boo-hoo! How did yer know I put it dere?"

Teacher: "Because you were the only boy in the room who was hard at work studying when I sat on it."

Johnny," said his teacher,
"if your father can do a piece of
work in seven days, and your
Uncle George can do it in nine
days, how long would it take
both of them to do it?"

"They'd never get it done," said
Johnny. "They'd sit down
and tell fish stories."

MOTHER: "What have you been doing so long?"

LITTLE DAUGHTER: "I heard papa say he was goin' to shave, so I thought I'd get all things ready for him."

"And did you?"

"Yes'm. I got out his razor and mug and shavin' brush and some court-plaster."

"Can you swim, little boy?"

"Yes, sir."

"Where did you learn?"

"In the water, sir."

First child (proudly): "My sister had a tooth pulled today, and she didn't make a bit of fuss about it."

Second Child (contemptuously): "Bah! That's nothing. My mamma takes all her teeth out every night and doesn't say a word about it."

Little Willie: "I wish I was you."

Mr. Selfmade (who has come to dinner): "And why, Willie?"

Little Willie: "'Cause you don't get your ears pulled for eatin' with your knife."

MAMMA: "Now, Teddy, we must all try and give up something while times are so hard."

TEDDY: "I'm willin.' "

MAMMA: "What will it be, dear?"

TEDDY: "Soap."

Georgie comes down to breakfast with a swollen visage, whereupon mamma says to the 4-year-old: "Why, Georgie, darling, don't you feel well? Tell mamma what is the matter."

Georgie (full of influenza): "No, I don't feel well. Bofe of my eyes is leakin' and one of my noses doesn't go."

Mother: "Did you take good care
of the parrot when I was
in the country, Tommy, and
not let it learn any bad words?"

Tommy: "Yes. I always took it
out of the room when Pa was
sewing on a button."

Farmer: *"Hang that cow!
I always have to club her 'fore
I can make her stand still."*

Little Nephew, from the city:
*"Is that the one that gives
the whipped cream?"*

Chapter Six

"Grandpa," asked the boy, "do hens make their own eggs?"

"Yes, they do," replied the old gentleman.

"And do they always put the yolk in the middle?"

"They do indeed, Johnny."

"And do they put the white around it to keep the yellow from rubbing off?"

"Er, quite likely."

"Then who sews the cover on?"

This stumped the old gentleman and he barricaded Johnny's mouth with a lollipop.

It's a Guy Thing

Bob: "I say, Sam, why did you
jilt her?"

Sam: "Oh, hang it, she lisped."

Bob: "Well, that's a charming defect
in a pretty girl."

Sam: "If you heard her say
Thweet Tham, instead of Sweet Sam,
you wouldn't wonder."

Bob: "Why, I never had any difficulty
that way. She always used to
call me darling Bob."

THE FLY THAT ONCE
THROUGH TARA'S HALLS,
WENT BUZZING SAD AND LONE,

NOW HAS A MYRIAD OF FRIENDS,
A FAMILY FULL GROWN.

AND WHEN OLD TARA FALLS ASLEEP,
ON EACH WARM SUMMER DAY,

THEY MEET ON HIS BALD PATE
AND DANCE,
TA-RA-RA BOOM-DE-AYE.

THE GLORIOUS FOURTH, I GRIEVE TO SAY,

DELIGHTS ME NOT LIKE OTHER MEN,

FOR I WAS MARRIED ON THAT DAY,

AND LOST MY INDEPENDENCE THEN.

*In speaking of the girl
to whom he was engaged,
he referred to her as
his "financee."*

*"You mean your fiancée,
I suppose? It is pronounced
feeahn-say."*

*"I don't care how it is
pronounced. This girl is my
financee. She is worth a
hundred thousand dollars."*

Wanted To Stay So

She: "If you are a professional woman-
hater, what are you going
to marry for?"

He: "So that I can live up to
my profession."

**"Are you ready to meet that
solemn event in every man's
existence, the new year?" asked
the meditative man.**

**"You bet I am," replied the
flippant friend. "I have more
material for swearing off than
I ever had in my life."**

Arthur: "I don't think she is pretty."

Jack: "Neither do I."

Arthur: "Heavens, she refused you, too."

Chummy: "What would you think of a man that always went around talking to himself?"

Gruffly: "I should say if he did it to listen to himself, he was a fool. If he did it to avoid listening to his friends, he was a genius. And if he did it to save his friends from listening to him, he was a philanthropist."

I I I

GUS DESMITH: "At the ball the other night you only danced once with Miss Esmeralda Longcoffin."

JOHNNIE MASHER: "I can't afford to encourage that girl. What do you think I smell whenever she is around?"

"Onions?"

"Worse than that. I smell orange blossoms. She means business, hence I must discourage her. She is not able to support a husband. How presuming the girls are getting nowadays."

Dicky Dummles: *"You have turned my brain all topsy-turvy, Miss Coldeal. (Tenderly) Can you read what is in my mind?"*

Miss Coldeal: *"I am afraid not, Mr. Dummles. I never could read upside down."*

A PENNY FOR YOUR THOUGHTS, SAID HE.

SHE SWEETLY SMILES, AS MAIDENS DO.

THEY ARE NOT WORTH THAT MUCH,
SAID SHE,

FOR I WAS THINKING, SIR, OF YOU.

Adversity has uses sweet,

And this one I do declare,

If you've a bald head,
soft and neat,

Your wife can never
pull your hair.

Carruthers: "I hear you are engaged to
one of the Rathburne twins. How do you
distinguish her from her sister?"

Waite: "Oh, prior to the wedding
I haven't regarded it as material, and
when the time comes I presume she will
know the difference."

AS SOON AS A MAN BECOMES
CONVINCED HE IS A GENIUS, THE FRINGE
SLOWLY BEGINS TO FORM ON THE BOTTOM
OF HIS TROUSERS.

*How do I know when a man's
a crank?*

It's easy to tell, said he,

*I always place a man
in that rank,*

When he doesn't agree with me.

"And what answer do you make to my appeal?" he asked as he knelt at her feet.

"James, I will be frank with you," she murmured.

"Oh, speak," he implored, "and relieve me from the agony of suspense."

"Then let me say it cannot be."

"Why not?"

"Because, James, I do not feel able to support a husband."

"If I'd known that I'd never have proposed in the first place."

Can You Marry an Epistle?

Bronco Bill: "What yer talkin' about makin' this here territory a state for? Yer can't make no state of it yet — 'tain't ready."

Alkali Ike: "Why ain't it, ye galoot?"

Bronco Bill: "Why ain't it, ye long-eared jackrabbit? Where yer goin' ter get yer United States senators? Ther ain't a man in the hull territory rich enough ter buy a ten-acre lot covered with pebbles!"

"It's no use arguing, my dear, I am going to give up my pew in church. I can't stand that new minister any longer."

"But, John — "

"But nothing, Maria. I haven't slept a wink for the last three Sunday mornings."

One of the very best of men,

No duty did he shirk,

Spent fifteen years in Congress,

then came home

and went to work.

Can You Marry an Epistle?

"And now, little girls," said the Sunday school teacher, "you may tell me about the epistles."

A little girl raised her hand.

"Well," said the teacher.

"The epistles," said the little girl, "are the wives of the apostles."

Fakerly: "Our standard of public morality is frightfully low."

Beezletop: "I'm afraid that too many of our legislators can be bought."

Fakerly: "Oh, no trouble about that! But you can't depend on the rascals when you have bought 'em."

"I UNDERSTAND YOU TRIED THE FAITH
CURE WITH SUCCESS."

"I DID. MY FAITH WAS CURED."

The stagecoach driver stopped outside
the saloon and alighted
in a cloud of dust. Hailing a
well-dressed pedestrian, he cried:

"Watch my coach
for a minute, will you?"

The well-dressed individual snorted
with rage. "Do you know that I am a
senator of this Territory?"

"Well, what of it," said the driver.
"I'll take a chance."

Little Johnny: *"Are you going to fire off crackers between your teeth?"*

Rev. Dr. Primrose: *"No, my young friend. I'm going to celebrate the glorious anniversary by delivering an oration. What put such a foolish idea into your head?"*

Little Johnny: *"I heard dad say you were going to shoot off your mouth."*

Judge: "How did the man libel you?

Applicant for warrant: "He called me a beggarly politician, yer honor."

Judge: "The word beggarly is hardly libelous."

Applicant for warrant: "It ain't that, yer honor. It's the word politician that I want satisfaction for."

Bad Eyesight Can Be Fatal

An old prospector just outside of a cave
announced that he had found a treasure
hidden inside.

"What is it, quartz?" he was asked.

"Naw," he whispered. "Pints."

HE STOOD ON THE STEPS AT MIDNIGHT
WITH WOBBLEDY, WOBBLEDY KNEE
AND WONDERED AND WONDERED
AND WONDERED
WHERE THE DAMNED KEYHOLE COULD BE.

Undertaker: "What kind of trimmings will you have on the coffin?"

Widow: "None whatever. It was trimmins that killed him."

Undertaker: "What?"

Widow: "Delirium trimmins."

First Moonshiner: "So ol' Si Plunkitt died mighty sudden, eh? What was the disease?"

Second Moonshiner: "Bad eyesight. He shot at a revenue officer and missed him."

*"Are you positive
the defendant was drunk?"*

*"No, doubt," growled
the constable.*

*"Why are you so almighty
certain about it?"*

*"Wall," replied the officer of the
law, "I saw him put a penny in
the patrol box, look up at the
clock on the Presbyterian
church and roar, 'Gawd! I've
lost fourteen pounds!'"*

125

Mrs. Rounder: "You had been drinking
pretty heavily when you
came in last night."

Mr. Rounder: "How do you know?"

Mrs. Rounder: "You tried to light
your cigar with the reflection of your
nose in the pier-glass."

**"Herbert," she said, "tell me
one thing, and tell me truthfully.
Were you ever intoxicated?"**

**"Well," replied the young man,
"I was air-tight once."**

"What do you mean?"

**"I had a tooth pulled and took
the laughing gas."**

Bilks: "Why did you
reprove me
for saying just now
that Soakers
drinks like a fish?"

Jilkers: "Because fish
don't drink more
than they need."

Mrs. Guzzleton: "You're not a bit superstitious, are you, John?"

Mr. Guzzleton: "Why, no, my dear. Why do you ask?"

Mrs. Guzzleton: "You came home last night when the clock would have struck thirteen if it could."

Saloon Man: *"Is O'Brien a good bluffer?"*

Second Saloon Man: *"No. Whenever he gets a spade he spits on his hands."*

Bad Eyesight Can Be Fatal

Employer: "I saw you coming out
of the saloon on the corner
three times today.
Don't let it occur again."

Clerk: "Last week you complained
because you saw me going
into the saloon. Now you complain
because you saw me coming out of it.
I don't seem to be
able to suit you, no how."

Women's Wit and Foibles

———◆━◆◆◆━◆———

Judge: "How old are you, miss?"

Elderly Female: "I am — I am
— I am — "

Judge: "Better hurry up. Every moment makes it worse."

Fanny: *"Who is that handsome fellow?"*

Maude: *"My intended."*

Fanny: *"Why, I didn't know you were engaged."*

Maude: *"I'm not."*

Chapter Ten

STELLA: "Wouldn't you
like to know that you
are the first girl
that Tom ever loved?"

ISABEL: "No. I'd rather be
certain that I'm the last one."

Gus DeSmith recently called
at the residence of the widow Flapjack.
The widow and her daughter, Lilly
Flapjack, received Gus in the parlor.

"Mr. DeSmith, don't you think
I resemble my mother?" asked Lilly.

"Lilly," said Mrs. Flapjack sharply,
"don't display your vanity
and egotism so much."

Miss Frank: "I believe in women's rights."

Mr. Cleverton: "Then you think every woman should have the vote?"

Miss Frank: "No. But I think every woman should have a voter."

Proprietor of shoe store: *"Before I take you into my employ as clerk, let me ask you one question: What do you know about the No. 2 size of ladies' shoes?"*

Applicant: *"There are seventeen sizes of No. 2 shoes."*

Proprietor: *"Hired!"*

I've a secret to disclose,

Sweet Marie,

It concerns your ruddy nose,

Sweet Marie,

It would soon come round
all right,

And once more be pearly white,

If you wouldn't lace so tight,

Sweet Marie.

"Tell me all," the pastor urged kindly.

"I put a button in the
contribution box," she faltered.

He smiled. "And did
your conscience trouble you?"

The woman raised her eyes earnestly.

"No," she answered. "I put in a wrong
button and broke a set, and I would
like to exchange it, if you please."

Prescilla: "I want to get
a gown to match
my complexion."

Perdita: "Why don't you get a
handpainted one?"

Kitty: *"We advanced women have discovered that man is a total failure."*

Tom: *"I suppose that is why you are claiming equality with him."*

**ONE WOMAN: "I think you
should feel utterly desolate
since your husband's death."**

**SECOND WOMAN: "Yes, indeed.
And yet it is a consolation
in knowing where
he spends his evenings."**

Passer: "What's going on
in that hall?"

Policeman: "Well, there's a lot of
long-haired men and short-haired
women there, but I don't know
whether it's a suffrage association
or an athletic club."

"How intelligent Melissa is."

**"Yes, she's homely,
isn't she?"**

*Girls and billiard balls
kiss each other with just about
the same amount of feeling.*

CAN A WOMAN A SECRET KEEP,

THERE IS ONE SUCH, I'LL ENGAGE,

AS THE YEARS UPON HER CREEP,

'TIS THE SECRET OF HER AGE.

"Did Miss Flyppe receive
many marriage proposals?"

"Many? Why, receiving
proposals has got to be a habit
with her. She has got so used to
them that she can't even
hear a soda water bottle pop
without exclaiming,
'This is so sudden!'"